Leighton Park
School

Great Ideals

LEIGHTON PARK SCHOOL AND
THE FIRST WORLD WAR

DREAMCATCHERS PUBLISHING

Leighton Park School
Shinfield Road,
Reading,
Berkshire.
RG2 7ED
UK

Dreamcatchers is a non-profit making venture, generously supported by the Leighton Park School Parent-Teacher Association.

First published May 2014

ISBN: 978-0-9566473-7-5

Printed in Reading, Berks by CONSERVATREE Print & Design, Ely Rd, Theale, Reading, West Berkshire RG7 4BQ.

FOREWORD

The Great War brought death and destruction to the world on an unprecedented scale. Over 8 million people were killed and 21 million wounded in this hellish conflict.

The world is made up of communities, and this book aims to tell the story of one of them – our school in the wartime years. What went on at the school? How did Leightonians respond to the call to serve their country? What was the guidance of the Society of Friends, and how much were Leightonians influenced by the Quaker ethos of the school? Who were these individual human beings whose names we see inscribed on the memorial tablet in Peckover?

To these factual questions answers can be found in this book, but the reader is led to reflect on deeper questions concerning the value of war and the desire for peaceful resolution of conflict, possible struggles between individual conscience and public pressure, on hypothetical questions about how one would have responded oneself in the circumstances of the First World War; perhaps most of all on the duty we have to live our own lives to the full, in pursuit of peace and goodness.

This book is a labour of love which John Allinson and Charlotte Smith have dedicated to the memory of all those members of our Leighton Park community whose lives were lost or badly affected in the First World War. It is a book for the heart and the mind, which, in thanking the authors and endorsing their aims, I commend to you.

Nigel Williams, Head.
April,2014

PREFACE

When we began our work on this short publication, our intentions were already clear. We wanted to tell the story of the impact of the First World War on the school and to record the different ways in which Old Leightonians answered the call to service in the War years. As our work has continued, we have felt drawn closer to these people – fellow human beings, fellow Leightonians – whose lives were so deeply affected, and in 28 cases, prematurely brought to an end, by the Great War. Our hope now is that the reader will have a share in the experience we have had of getting to know some men who once worked and played at this school, who enjoyed the serenity and beauty of the Park, but whose lives were blighted by the War.

'What would I have done?' is a question that presents itself to us, who have never had to face the dilemma of whether or not to enlist in the Armed Forces and fight for our country. We hope that this book will give the reader cause for reflection. It is so easy to think of something that happened a hundred years ago as no longer relevant to our lives. That, it seems to us, is far from being the case.

The inscription on the school's First World War memorial board reads 'They died for great ideals'. Great ideals inspired those who fought in the War and those whose conscience did not allow them to fight. Great ideals, deeply rooted in the Quaker values of the school, were surely also motivating the staff and the pupils as they did their best to live honourably and diligently at Leighton Park in the wartime years.

John Allinson and Charlotte Smith

FRIENDS AND ENEMIES

Quakers are deeply committed to the pursuit of peace, and many hold that it is unchristian to engage in warfare. They believe that, since there is that of God in everyone, to kill or injure a fellow human being would be to reject the sanctity of life and thereby offend God. The 1660 statement to King Charles II by a small group of early Quakers, including the recognised founder, George Fox, contains these seminal and uncompromising words:

All bloody principles and practices, we, as to our own particulars, do utterly deny, with all outward wars and strife and fightings with outward weapons, for any end or under any pretence whatsoever.

The outbreak of the First World War was an enormous challenge to Quakers. There were those who felt that the atrocities that had precipitated the war and the scale of the threat to civilisation were enough to justify signing up for the Armed Forces. It was as if the Peace Testimony was now in abeyance – a set of ideals that were put on hold while the expedient business of fighting a just war was undertaken. The Society of Friends did not prevent its members from following their conscience in this way, however abhorrent it considered war to be.

Those who did not join up of their own volition faced conscription when the Military Service Act was introduced in January 1916. Of the 1100 Friends who applied for exemption as conscientious objectors, nearly 300 were imprisoned, in most cases because they were 'absolutists', i.e. they refused to do any form of alternative work to help the war effort. Though prison conditions were harsh, those serving sentences were at least luckier than the 34 objectors, including 3 Quakers, who were sent to France and suffered the shock of being sentenced to death for persistently disobeying orders. Their sentences were commuted to ten years' hard labour after sentence was pronounced.

A major source of advice and exhortation for Quakers was the weekly magazine 'The Friend'. It was days after the declaration of war in August 1914 that this seminal message from the Religious Society of Friends was published:

Our duty is clear: to be courageous in the cause of love and in the hate of hate…….. While as a Society we stand firmly to the belief that the method of force is no solution of any question, we hold that the present moment is not one for criticism, but for devoted service to our nation. In the sight of God we should seek to get back to first principles, and to determine on a course of action which shall prove us to be worthy citizens of His Kingdom.

Throughout the war the magazine included a section entitled 'Some thoughts on the present situation'. What, it asked, was the role of a Quaker amidst the havoc and horror of war? How could the pacifist Quaker still play a part in society and, indeed, avoid being misunderstood and thought of as idle or cowardly? Would it be acceptable for a Quaker to take up arms? These extracts speak for themselves:

How can we translate, or at least represent our peace testimony in time of war? The answer to these hard questions must be made but each one for himself….. no man can answer for another.

The peaceable spirit in wartime is courageous in love and reveals itself in avoidance of hatred, of lust, of spoliation, of glorification, arrogance and revenge, of jingoism in all its forms and of all the vices which tend to accompany war; it reveals itself also in a new appreciation of Discipline, Devotion to duty, Endurance and Self-Sacrifice.

It is said that the day when our Quaker ideals can be thought of as practical politics is too remote to call for consideration………….we are little better than hypocrites, living a protected and comfortable life because, fortunately for us, there are brave soldiers and sailors whose sacrifices we accept as our

safeguard....... We must guard against presumptuous sin, against spiritual pride, inconsistent profession and personal selfishness.
(The Friend, 11th September 1914)

In the 18th September 1914 edition, an important characteristic of Quaker values is addressed: the right and, indeed, responsibility of the individual to make his own choices. Nevertheless, unequivocal guidance is also given as to the right choice!

Our view is that it is a principle of Quakerism that the individual shall himself seek for guidance as to what line of action he shall pursue, and having found his path, that he shall follow it faithfully, courageously and even with joy. We find it difficult to conceive of a true Quaker enlisting as a soldier, but even that action we should be careful to judge. The taking of the life of another seems to be the negation of Quakerism, which heightens the value of human life.

One third of eligible Quakers enlisted for military service.

In some cases, they found the experience of warfare so abhorrent that they tried to change their minds on the grounds of conscientious objection – easier said than done. One such man, later to become renowned for his peace work and study of ornithology, was Horace Alexander. War, he said was *'the most stupid and ridiculous barbarism ever invented'*. His personal experience of it was to change him for ever. In a face to face encounter with a German soldier, he had run his knife through him and killed him, but then, instead of advancing with his group, he looked back at the body of the man he had killed:

'I fell down beside him, and all my manhood or hardihood gave way. I went and sobbed over him. I saw that he had a pale and sorrowful face, gentle and kind.'

Quakers were the foremost religious organisation in the denunciation of war, though, of course, there were others who held similar views. In an essay entitled 'What is the duty of the Christian citizen?' the committed Christian pacifist and politician Dr Alfred Salter challenged his readers to ask themselves if they could imagine *'Christ in khaki, thrusting his bayonet into the body of a German workman.'*

The two main channels for Quaker relief work were the Friends Ambulance Unit (FAU) and the War Victims Relief Committee (WVRC) . Though of a non-combatant nature, their work was intense and often dangerous. Sir George Newman, Chairman of the Friends Ambulance Unit, wrote in 1919:

The best of these men possessed the fighter's daring, the wise man's understanding of his duty, the good man's self-discipline in its performance. They also had a pleasant and sustaining fund of good humour which brightened the dark hours of their own life and that of thousands of others…. The best of them, like the best soldiers……yielded their lives as a willing offering on its (the Commonwealth) behalf. The best of them knew….. the secret of happiness is service and freedom, and the secret of freedom a brave heart.

LEIGHTON PARK: A WARTIME OASIS

A superficial reading of 'The Leightonian' and other school records might lead one to conclude that the school continued to function as normal, unaffected by – perhaps even oblivious and indifferent to – the War.   The school had its own life – a routine of unremarkable, humdrum days alternating with noteworthy events like plays, Sports Days, concerts, 'rags', staff socials and even spectacularly scurrilous pranks.

But this would be an erroneous, even unfair conclusion. A more suitable interpretation would be that the school responded to Charles Evans's appeal to approach all aspects of their work assiduously and to avoid the temptations of inertia and self-indulgence. In the April 1916 edition of the 'Leightonian' we read:

We at the school may be said to be 'carrying on'. The football season has been a successful one; the Societies meeting in the new Library have issued excellent reports, and, as we write, training for the Sports is in full swing. And yet things are not quite the same. The horror of the conflict turns our thoughts constantly in the direction of the War. We hope that the interchange of ideas, the endeavour to understand all points of view, and the sense of our responsibility in the future, will materially add to our equipment, enable us to take our place as useful citizens when the time comes for us to leave school.

One former pupil of that period, R.A.U.Jennings, commented:

School life in the early war years was school life and not war life. For this and countless other things we may be grateful to Charles Evans: in his bearing and in his teaching and his Sunday evening addresses he was always 'on top of' the War, and it cannot have been easy.

The Headmaster did indeed play a crucial role throughout the War, and some would say that the guidance he gave at the outset was one of his greatest interventions:

We have been brought sharply up against the possibilities of good and evil, and have been met by an unexpected and urgent call that has left none of us where it found us............But at the same time sympathy is called out more especially to OLs who have arrived at an age to make their own decisions. ... There are, I believe, OLs wearing khaki today to whom War is abhorrent. Many another finds himself unable, for conscience sake, to join in war at all, and has to turn to other ways of helping his country and humanity. I rejoice that outlets have been found for the zeal of some of these in work in Belgium and France. I rejoice still more at the constancy and courage that our non-combatants are maintaining.

Whilst acknowledging the right of individuals to make their own mind up, he was clear in his own stance:

It is an augury of hope that so many Leightonians, teachers and taught, find themselves more sure than ever that all war is opposed to the spirit and teaching of Jesus Christ, and that this war is no exception.

Expressing his thankfulness for all true effort that the War called out from Leightonians, he said:

What would be grievous hearing is that a Leightonian is indifferent, or embittered or a scoffer.

The Leightonian editorial of December 1914 shows that the school was trying hard to deliver normal service as far as possible, but was far from forgetting what was happening in the outside world:

It is impossible even in a school magazine to avoid reference to the War. To a certain extent it is true that we have pursued the even tenor of our way, both in our work and games, and yet it is equally true that the human suffering involved and the self-sacrifice displayed had greatly affected our outlook. History has become more real to us, now that we see it in the making; strategy and tactics have given a lively interest to geography, and the meetings of the Debating Society and the LHA have, we are sure, helped many of us to form sound ideas as to the origin of this awful strife and the possibilities of a lasting peace.

Before the War had broken out, the school's governing board (then known as the Directors of the Public School Company) had realised that the school had to increase its number on roll to survive. An extensive building programme – the 1914 Scheme - was approved, but the construction of the Central Buildings (now known as Peckover) was not finally signed off until September. The War was already underway, and questions arise as to the incongruousness of this apparent self-indulgence. Insofar as one can determine, however, the War was not expected to last more than a few weeks and the School building project provided employment to local people. The minutes of the Governors' meetings of that time reveal, nevertheless, that instructions were given to avoid any extravagance in the design and construction of the building.

Materials needed for the construction of the new Central Buildings were transported from the front gate by a light railway across Grove Field – it was a source of much enjoyment to the boys.

Another way in which money was saved was the deployment of child labour! Working in teams and equipped with pick and shovel, the pupils had to dig the sunken fence, now more commonly referred to as the ha-ha, to keep out the sheep and protect the view across the park in preparation for the new Central Building.

In 1915 the boys became increasingly involved in work related to the war. Many boys had already been following ambulance training courses and helping refugees. The school became involved in the making of splints for the war wounded. Social events were reduced so that more time could be devoted to the task of producing 300 splints per week – one hundred each of leg, arm and hand splints.

In summer 1915, The Leightonian reported that many pupils would be working as volunteers during the holidays on fruit gathering and haymaking:

'Let everyone return in September with the satisfaction that he has given some of his leisure time to the nation'

In the event, 40 pupils from a number of Quaker schools had worked at Evesham in Worcestershire. A 4.45 am wake-up call ensured they were ready for their working day, from 6am to 5 pm.

The opening of the gracious and dignified new Central Buildings was a cause of celebration in the autumn of 1915. Normal school life continued: staff meeting discussions on such matters as whether or not to allow whistling in the new building; concerts, lectures, often illustrated by lantern slides, on such edifying topics as 'Medieval Walled Towns' and 'Methods of Attacking the Drink Problem' ; sports, skating on the pond, the introduction of Esperanto to the hobbies programme; the occasional excitement such as that caused by the reported night-time discovery of a German spy on the Park, or the fire in the roof of the farm buildings, extinguished by heroic members of staff before the fire brigade arrived.

Visits from the Friends Ambulance Unit, which had a training centre at Jordans, near Beaconsfield, were a source of fun and companionship, not least because some OLs were in the party. Football matches were the order of the day, but the FAU also used the school grounds for some serious training. On one occasion, the unit spent the night practising the skills of searching for casualties and administering first aid.

There were regular talks at the school on the FAU, and on the Friends War Relief Committee, and pupils and staff did some valuable work locally with refugees and aliens. There was a concentration camp for German internees at Newbury Racecourse, and groups of LP staff and pupils would visit them and enjoy concerts, sport and conversation quite regularly. Similarly, help was given setting up and managing 'Sutherlands', a house for 40 Belgian Refugees in Christchurch Road.

The newly established J.B. Hodgkin Elocution Competition was the arena for a number of speeches connected with the War, including 'England's Duty of Disarmament', 'Conscientious Objection'. The topic of the war was never far from the preoccupations of the Debating Society. Already in the

Autumn term of 1914 the Debating Society was debating the motion 'That in the opinion of this house, the Allies ought to make peace as soon as Germany offers'. It was defeated by nine votes to fifteen. The reader may be similarly surprised to know that a motion 'that in the opinion of this house the Government is justified in making all Germans prisoners of war' was carried by 11 votes to 3. Later, however, a motion deprecating the calls for the introduction of conscription was carried by 15 votes to 5, and one calling for the sale and consumption of alcohol during wartime was carried emphatically. On 27 November 1915 there was a joint debate with Reading School Debating Society. J.B. Fryer and R.A.U. Jennings proposed the motion that war brings more harm than good in its train. It was carried by 24 votes to 10.

The most remarkable meeting of the Debating Society took place on 23 October 1916. It took the form of a Military Tribunal session, in which 8 members, playing the roles of people from various backgrounds, set forth their cases for exemption from conscription. The brief record of this meeting indicates that lengthy consideration was given to their often complicated cases. *'Speeches, interesting, with fervid thoughts aglow, at times marred by irrelevancy'* opined the 'Leightonian' s correspondent.

In 1916, the shortage of labour led to all boys being expected to put in at least one hour of manual labour per week, under the supervision of

prefects. Much of this was in the form of efforts to increase food production – digging up ground on the Park, in local allotments and private gardens. 20 senior boys would be seen working in this way on any day of the week.

Reading Borough Council expressed appreciation of their help. The least popular activity was breaking up the hard earth between the sanatorium and the fives' court. 21st century readers may need to consult an old plan of the school to see where this was! During this period, the games programme was curtailed and the House Challenge Shield suspended.

The end of the War on 11th November 1918 was marked by the loud pealing of bells - the first sound of the bells since they had been silenced in 1916. There was a short meeting for everyone on the estate and an ad hoc social in the evening. Charles Evans gave an address in which, after a deeply moving remembrance of the school's dead, spoke of the wider significance of the Armistice Commemoration and of how it must be the earnest endeavour of all men of good will to make future wars impossible. The main Peace Celebrations were held in July 1919, including a fête, sports, a 'masque', an obstacle race for cyclists, a boat trip to Marlow and a jolly sing-song on the way back.

One inevitable consequence of the war was the depleted attendance at the annual reunions of Old Leightonians. In June 1914, 75 former pupils had come to the school for their usual gathering. The numbers dropped during the war years, but the strong bonds of Leightonian friendship were not to be broken that easily. The following chapters show only too clearly why it was difficult to maintain these friendships, but somehow many former pupils kept in touch.

A striking example of this spirit of Leightonian camaraderie is the extraordinary occasion which reunited OL members of the FAU for a dinner at a hotel near Dunkirk on 28th July 1917. At the same time, the annual gathering of OLs was taking place at Leighton Park, and it was from there that the Dunkirk party received a telegram:

Fifteen Old Leightonians, staff and school, greet fifteen Old Leightonians abroad. HODGKIN

Gervase Ford, in his report of the occasion, wrote:

The gathering under such different surroundings to the usual OL meetings will ever remain in the memories of those who were present at a momentous occasion of a reunion in the war-zone of the Great War.

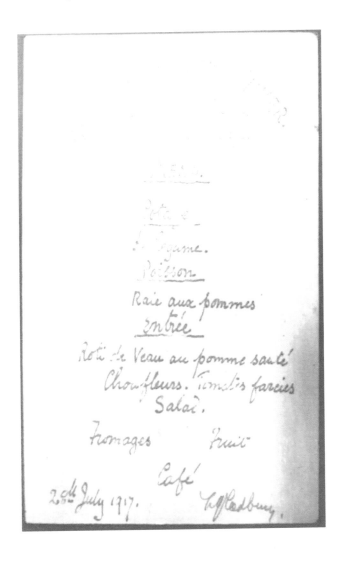

LEIGHTONIANS IN KHAKI

We have been able to find information about 200 of the 300 Leightonians who would have faced the dilemma of deciding whether or not to serve in the Armed Forces. Of this number, we have calculated that 65% enlisted in the Armed Forces, whilst 35% did not enlist. Most of the latter were engaged in some form of relief work, recorded in the next section of this book.

Those who chose military service were not subject to criticism from the Society of Friends in general or from the school. On recording the first deaths of OLs, the Leightonian remarks unequivocally:

Our sorrow and sympathy is mingled with pride when we remember that they followed the path of duty, regardless of consequences.

In total, 28 Leightonians lost their lives during the First World War, and at least 50 were wounded. To the list of fatalities we must add the name of Erskine Crossley, who was severely injured in the War and died in 1920 of pneumonia. It is dreadful to think of their deaths and injuries, and indeed to think of the families who must have been devastated to receive the terrible news. What words of comfort would suffice in the case of Archie Warner's family? He was one of three sons to be killed in action.

Every single death of a Leightonian, indeed of any human being, during the War was, of course, a catastrophic tragedy, but one feels it even more acutely in the case of Clive Thorpe. He was killed by a shell three days before the end of the War. Whilst we ourselves can be thankful that we are living in an era removed in time from the trauma of the First World War, we can spare a thought for Thorpe. He nearly made it, but he was never to know the joy and elation of Armistice Day.

C.S. Richmond wrote to the Headmaster in March 1916, providing a vivid description of his experiences with the 16th Middlesex at the front. His account, though a record of terrible suffering and discomfort, has touches of humour and understatement which, dare I say, feel very 'Leightonian'.

About 25 of us are now tucked away (with a very undesirable dog as a companion) in a small barn with crumbly mud walls and a very antiquated roof through which at night we are able to study the stars at our leisure, and through which at other times we are unable to enjoy a delightful cold douche.

They were resting and fairly comfortable compared with what they had just left:

We were about 75 yards from our friend the enemy and about six to eight inches under the snow; this lasted well over a week. The shelters were totally inadequate to our needs and sleep in such a temperature was of course rendered impossible; while villainously dark and foggy nights left our nerves a complete wash-out after a few days of it. The slippery frozen trenches made it extremely difficult for carrying rations up the line, and as a consequence we suffered additionally from lack of food. The cold was intense, but notwithstanding this, Fritz was fairly active with hand-grenades and trench mortars…………In several places we have been up to the waist in water and liquid mud for days on end without a dry rag in our possession…………I had one or two near things just recently; in one case a heavy trench mortar came and fell in the next traverse to me, blew in the trench all around, burying several men; one dug-out was blown in with a man inside. While three of us dug the men out they dropped about half a dozen more heavy mortars round us; only two of us came out untouched.

Denis Gilford was awarded the Military Medal following unselfish acts of heroism as a stretcher-bearer in the midst of battle:

Soon after 4.30 am the biggest barrage on record began. I was right up on the Ridge. There I dressed Lance-Corporal Street, who had a broken leg. Soon after I had a man with a bullet through the lung. Just as I was dressing him, Fritz counter-attacked from behind the flank. Soon after that I had a call from a Jock. Two men had been killed and three wounded trying to get one of our men in. Not thinking at all, I rushed out and lay down by him. He had an arm and a leg broken, and the other leg wounded. As we were under fire I pulled him on my back and got in as fast as I could. Later, I had the first food and drink for over 50 hours. The worst of it was that Fritz was using explosives and poisoned bullets and was picking off the stretcherbearers and the wounded. I was very lucky indeed: one bullet broke a lens in my glasses, another broke the side wire, another knocked a cigarette out of my mouth, and another, an explosive one, tore my trousers and burst against something behind me! You will guess how thankful I was to get out untouched.

Surgeon-Lieutenant William Fryer Harvey was awarded the Albert Medal for his act of great gallantry at sea. When two torpedo-boat destroyers collided he was sent on board the more seriously damaged destroyer to assist the injured. A petty officer was pinned by the arm in a damaged compartment. With the boiler room flooded and full of fumes from the escaping oil, and minutes to go before the ship was to break in two, Harvey remained on board to perform an amputation of the officer's arm, thereby saving him from certain death. Harvey collapsed at the end of the operation and had to be hauled out of the boat.

Although one or two other Leightonians had been prisoners of war, the longest period was endured by Alan Gilford, who had been interred in Holland for nine months and then imprisoned in Germany for over 3 years.

Amidst the accounts of the injuries, fatalities and the general wretchedness of the wartime experiences, we find in the pages of 'The Leightonian' some heartening records of more positive and even entertaining experiences. One of these is a witness to Old Leightonians' affection for their alma

: ENNEMAIN — Le Château — P. D.

mater. When two OL officers of the Berkshire regiment were billeted in an old château in France, they renamed it Leighton Park. It was revisited during the war years by other Leightonians. They were former member of staff Capt. Whittaker and John A (Jack) Brain. They were members of the 'C' Company of the Royal Berkshire Regiment, and, in March 1917, they arrived at the little village of Ennemain, from which the Germans had recently retreated to the other side of the Somme. Before leaving they had practically destroyed the village and set fire to its château. Many men in the battalion came from Reading, and as they set about the task of repairing the roads they enjoyed renaming the village streets 'Broad Street' 'The Butts', etc. Whittaker and Brain erected a large board four feet square on which was painted the name 'Leighton Park' they placed it at the front entrance of the château.

We close this chapter with an image of wartime medals and the extraordinary tale that goes with them. As we write, one hundred years after the Great War began and a few years since the death of the last surviving 'Tommies', we have just received as a gift from his 105 year-old widow, the wartime medals of an OL, A.L. Braithwaite. He served in both

20

the First and the Second World Wars. We thank Mrs Joan Braithwaite for entrusting us with the care of these medals.

OUT OF THE FRYING-PAN—

Pathetic plight of unconscientious conscientious objector who learns in the Press that he may be put on to mine-sweeping

SURELY the War Prophets might decently retire on their war profits, and leave us to the honest facts, which are bad enough in all conscience.

※ ※

MR. GEORGE has taken over the Metropole as a solatium. It is understood that he would have preferred Buckingham Palace. But the Metropole has its advantages. Politically, it is half-way between the National Liberal and Constitutional Clubs, and it will be equally easy for Mr. George to wobble to either the one or the other. Also, it is a very costly building, and is, consequently, in keeping with the spendthrift traditions of his office. But what in the world are they going to do with all the bedrooms? *And* the cellars?

'I DARE NOT TAKE ANY MAN'S LIFE'

Mankind must put an end to war, or war will put an end to mankind... War will exist until that distant day when the conscientious objector enjoys the same reputation and prestige that the warrior does today." John F Kennedy

Conscientious objectors attracted derision and opprobrium rather than prestige in First World War Britain. The white feathers mockingly given to male civilians by some women came to symbolise the incomprehension, scorn and resentment.

Nevertheless, true to their pacifist principles, a good number of Old Leightonians accepted war relief work instead of joining up for the armed services. In some cases, this meant working for the Friends' Ambulance Unit. It has been said that such work involved a very high level of risk in that the volunteers were frequently required to be on the front line. Others were fully engaged in essential war relief work.

Laurence Angus wrote about work with the *Société des Amis* in Eastern France following heavy fighting. The organisation was initially treated with suspicion but soon became as trusted as the Croix Rouge. Indeed, two Old Leightonians received the *Croix de* Guerre for courageous actions in ambulance convoys. Angus began by commenting on the way nature was recovering from the heavy battles, but then turned to the more complex needs of the people.

Over the broad mounds of French and German graves is spreading a veil of new grass. The spade marks are less noticeable in the trenches; the ration

24

tins are rusting out of sight. The soft south winds bring gentler sounds than the rumble of guns.

The part that remains for man to do is almost appallingly great. Even where their house has not been burned or destroyed by shells, the people have lost a great deal by pillage - sheets, clothing, food, wine, cattle. Women who can use their needle are reduced to sewing themselves garments from soldiers' shirts off the battlefield. We cannot lose sight of the tragedy that is implied in that. How far does the furnishing of roof and clothing help to relieve the mental stress there must be. Some of the old people have succumbed to the shock; women widowed by the war have nothing but the ruins of their homes to face. Even energetic men seem staggered by their losses.

E.F. Wills sent a detailed account of his work on a Friends Ambulance train. He writes of the nervous time spent in a railway siding while waiting to load up the train with wounded soldiers. A fierce strafing has been going on throughout the night, and the train rocks violently at each loud burst of bombs and gunfire. The first job is to decide where to place each wounded soldier and to make them comfortable before they are seen by a doctor.

'Here down below is a poor fellow with a broken thigh, suffering intensely; he seems to be alternately laughing and cursing... here is a mere boy with a shrapnel wound in his head; he has brought his steel helmet with him, without which he would have been killed. Above him there is a man with trench feet – a common enough complaint.... and so I go through the ward until I come to the twentieth and last patient. He has shrapnel wound in his chest, and was the sole survivor of six. With difficulty he tells his story, but it all has to be dragged out. Suddenly I discover he comes from my town: the barrier disappears. Everyone is anxious to know the destination, but we are not told. It appears that we have missed our 'marche' and will have to wait two hours before proceeding to the next station for further loading. An R.A.M.C. bearer thinks that another bombardment is about to take place.

Conscientious objectors could be roughly divided into two groups – those who refused to bear arms but would undertake other non-military tasks, and those who refused any form of involvement which could be construed as helping the war effort. All who applied for exemption had to face a military tribunal. The tribunal officials needed a lot of persuading as to the purity of the applicants' motives, but membership of the Society of Friends normally increased the likelihood of a sympathetic hearing.

Walter Alan Peaslake Bell claimed exemption from military service and refused non-combatant work as his conscience told him there was no difference between that and going to fight. As a Christian, he said, his highest allegiance was to God. When asked what would happen to the country if everyone was a Christian like him, Walter Bell replied that if everybody lived up to the Christian ideal, war was an impossibility. The Chairman remarked that it was a pity the Kaiser did not belong to Walter Bell's sect (The Society of Friends) and he dismissed his application.

Joseph Bigland Fryer's appeal for absolute exemption at Auckland rural Tribunal in County Durham was successful; technically, Government regulations obliged the Chairman to exempt him as he was a Quaker and was accepted by the Friends Ambulance Unit. His plea for exemption, based on the teachings of Jesus Christ, was also taken into account:

All men are brethren, and the individual soul, however debased it may seem, is capable of such an infinite amount of good that I dare not take any man's life; the only true method of changing the evil mind of men is by trust in them and love of them. The evaluation of that statement is as relevant now in the 21st century as it was then.

Joseph Fryer died tragically shortly after the War, and the school's Fryer House, formerly the Hospice, was given in his memory.

Eric P Southall served three prison sentences. The first was 112 days' hard labour in Winson Green Prison, Birmingham and included periods of solitary confinement. Then followed a spell in Wormwood Scrubs, having refused to wear khaki and strip for medical inspection. He was given a third sentence to be served at Dorchester Prison, from where he wrote to the school to say that he was being treated quite well and to express his hope that Leighton Park would turn out more pacifists.

The depressing business of being held on remand while awaiting court martial is described at the beginning of Lyn Harris's account of his experiences in 'The Leightonian' of December 1917.

'Guard, take these prisoners to the guard-room and place them under close arrest!'

Tramp, tramp we go: up a dirty passage, three flights of increasingly dirty stairs, then into a small, dingy attic, the only light coming from a window at one end. A dirty cupboard serving as a place of concealment for several doubtful blankets, and the remnants of repasts, is open in the corner. We are searched and left alone in the slow-gathering darkness. Even light is forbidden, but someone discovers a bit of candle and secretly lights it; every now and then it is extinguished when the alarm of a surprise is raised.

In the next few days, examinations by officers – the chief disagreeableness consists of the continual abuse and insult. The cold is horrible and life is one long chilliness.

Eventually, the group is tried by court martial and their prison sentence is read out with full pomp and ceremony.

Basil Bunting, widely regarded as one of Britain's most important twentieth century poets, was an absolutist conscientious objector. The reports of his tribunal illustrate that he was an assertive and confident defender of his position, so much so that he astounded the tribunal officials and the local press with his remarks. One local newspaper ran their report of the tribunal with the headline *Newcastle 'Conchy' Would Sooner See Huns Over-running Country than Kill a Man.*

Suffice it to say that there was not a meeting of minds between Bunting and the tribunal panel member, future Conservative MP George Renwick:

Renwick: You would rather stay here and let other men die for you in France?
Bunting: Yes
Renwick: You are a beauty, you are!

 Bunting spent several months in Wormwood Scrubs Prison, making mailbags and twisting ships' fenders. He had hospital treatment for a septic ulcer, and then, having refused to obey an order, he was court-martialled a second time and sent to do hard labour at Winchester Prison. He went on hunger strike and was eventually released in June 1919.

Ronald Lloyd, one of four sons, returned from a cricket tour in 1914 and immediately faced the dilemma of whether or not to sign up for military service.

My parents were very good about it. They left it to each of us to decide. They said you do what you feel to be right about it.

He joined the FAU. No sooner had he completed his training that he and his group were sent to France. On the way there, they had to interrupt their journey to treat victims of the torpedo attack on 'Hermes'. It was an early introduction to the horrors of war.

The relief work in France called for vigour and commitment, and at times great courage was called for and shown. The correspondent of a French newspaper paid this tribute to him:

Day and night he ran in under heavy shell fire to get the people out of the cellars and falling houses. In addition to this he carried hundreds of wounded soldiers, and was always the first to get them back to safety.

A retired colonel wrote to FAU Headquarters:

If your men had been in the Army, four of them at least would have earned a VC.

In spite of the great danger to which he was exposed, Lloyd felt increasingly that he was 'skulking behind the Army' and that he was in comparative comfort. He felt compelled to enlist in the Armed Forces, and he joined the Field Artillery in December 1917.

A TALE OF TWO CADBURYS

The brothers Egbert and Laurence Cadbury reacted to the onset of war in very different ways. Bertie (Egbert) could hardly wait to join the Royal Navy. He later wrote that he thought the war would be over by Christmas and feared that unless he was quick he would miss all the fun.

Laurence was implacably opposed to fighting and he became a key member of the Friends Ambulance Unit.

Bertie was an undergraduate at Trinity College, Cambridge when war broke out. His letters describing his experiences in the Navy reveal his courage, and maybe a touch of feigned or even actual nonchalance:

Yesterday we visited a minefield of ill repute and there sunk numerous mines. One mine exploded practically under our counter and a piece struck me violently on the arm, luckily not inflicting any injury.

In 1915 he joined the Royal Naval Air Service and within a few days of completing his training at Great Yarmouth he flew his first mission to attack German Zeppelins. The Zeppelins were very elusive, and none was shot down for over a year, in which time 20 raids were made, 207 civilians killed and 573 injured.

Bertie's attempts to shoot down a Zeppelin were thwarted on two or three occasions. On 23rd September 1916 the Zeppelins were attacking and Bertie patrolled for 2½ hours at 7000 feet but saw nothing and had to land for fuel. Shortly afterwards he saw a Zeppelin flying through the spot he had been patrolling. '*I do have sickening luck*' he commented.

His luck changed a month later when he shot down his first Zeppelin, a feat for which he was awarded the DSC. He assumed greater responsibility at the airfield. At the formation of the RAF he was appointed Captain and put in charge of a squadron.

His vivid description of the dramatic shooting down of a Zeppelin in 1918 is redolent of stories in the 'Boys' Own' magazines of last century. The danger and the excitement seem to have been great motivators for Bertie. On the evening of 5th May he was listening to his girl-friend Mary singing at a charity concert when he was alerted to the fact that German Zeppelins were heading towards the area. His haste to be up in the air in the thick of the fight is remarkable:

Knowing that there was only one machine available with the necessary speed and climb…. I roared down to the station in an ever-ready Ford, seized a scarf, goggles and helmet, tore off my streamline coat, and, semi-clothed with a disreputable jacket under my arm, sprinted as hard as ever Nature would let me, and took a running jump into the pilot's seat. I beat my most strenuous competitor by one-fifth of a second. Once in the seat, I knew that, given a reasonable amount of luck, I should certainly destroy one, if not three of the intruders.

He and his gunner, flying at 16,000 ft in the night sky, located one of the Zeppelins, fired at it, and saw it plunge seaward as a blazing mass. They had destroyed the L70, regarded as the finest Zeppelin in existence. It had on board Peter Strasser, the Chief of the German Airship Service, as well as a crew of 14. Their attempt to annihilate a second Zeppelin narrowly failed, and, with the engine intermittently cutting out and the main gun blocked, they gave up the chase.

'I was lost. I think that half-hour, diving through 12,000 feet of cloud in inky blackness on a machine that I had been told could not land at night, even if I made land again, was the most terrible I have ever experienced.'

On landing, he discovered that the two 110-lb bombs he thought he had ditched early in the flight were still attached. The plane could so easily have crashed and caught fire.

Bertie and his gunner Robert Leekie were awarded the Distinguished Flying Cross. They were guests of honour at a celebratory party, and it is reported that Bertie was carried on a chair shoulder-high through the streets of Yarmouth, clearly idolised by the local population.

Bertie wrote to his father:

Another Zeppelin has gone to destruction, sent there by a perfectly peaceful, 'live and let live' citizen, who has no lust for blood of fearful war spirit in his veins. It all happened very quickly and very terribly.

Laurence, the eldest of the six children of George Cadbury and his second wife, Elizabeth Taylor, chose to join the Friends Ambulance Unit. More accurately, he helped found it, with Philip Noel-Baker and a few other Quakers. He stayed with the unit from September 1914 to March 1919.

For the first two years he was in charge of an ambulance convoy, known as a Section Sanitaire Anglaise, which consisted of 20 ambulances and 56 men. In 1916 he was moved to the FAU Headquarters in Malo, near Dunkirk, where he became the Officer in charge of transport.

He took his own car to use as an ambulance in France, for there was, at least initially, a shortage of vehicles.

Laurence Cadbury committed himself indefatigably to the varied relief work which the Unit undertook, particularly in and around Ypres.

In his regular letters home, he described some of the intensely demanding work he had to do – in one week, he transported 905 wounded people, in many cases having personally extracted them from rubble while under shell fire. In a vivid description of shell attacks on Ypres hospital, he notes that he and other FAU members were lucky to escape injury when so many others were killed or wounded. This happened repeatedly.

In the later years of the War, Laurence became increasingly concerned that he was not doing his bit for Britain, and that he should join the Armed Forces. In a note to himself he listed the reasons for changing, including the shame he would feel as a non-combatant when he returned to England. His father did much to persuade him to stay with the FAU, robustly refuting his arguments:

Your friends are in the army – and some have died – and you think they are doing much more than you. They, knowing your position, think the same of you; and there can be no question that everyone here thinks of you in the highest terms

Egbert and Laurence had different characters and different experiences, but in terms of their vigour, their strength and their perseverance, they were very much alike.

THE MEN BEHIND THE MEMORIAL

In the following pages the reader will find descriptions of those former pupils who died – brief notes on brief lives.

In many cases, the words are quoted from entries in 'The Leightonian' magazine.

Encapsulated in this cv format with its aptly named bullet points are the short and promising lives of young men who had everything to live for but who died so heartbreakingly young.

G. Ll. Hodgkin

Full name: George Lloyd Hodgkin
Years at L.P: 1892-1898
House: Grove
Date of birth: 22/08/1880
Higher education: Natural Sciences at Trinity College Cambridge
Position in military: conscientious objector
Date of death: 24/06/1918 (aged 37)
Reason for death: dysentery

At Leighton Park
- School Sport: Captain of the 1st XI football team ,tennis team, cricket team
- Societies: Assistant secretary of the Essay Society, and President of the Debating Society
- Debating Society 1897: "On Saturday 27th of February, we read *As You Like It*, instead of having a debate. Celia's part was admirably read by George Hodgkin."
- Football: "G. Ll. Hodgkin has made a good captain. His combined play with Ford has been the feature of our attack."

- "The essay "The Greek City of Akragas" by G. Ll. Hodgkin was an uncommon paper in which the author had compiled with success, information entirely unknown to his hearers."
- At the Music Society's 1897 annual Musical Evening on Saturday the 24th of July, George played two flute solos: "Hodgkin made a commendable first appearance as a solo flautist."

Post Leighton Park
- Trinity College Cambridge Exhibition (£40 per annum)
- "We would congratulate G. Ll. Hodgkin on his having successfully passed his first exams. In the exuberance of his joy he has been seen brandishing a rattle. This, we would hasten to inform O.L's, is neither a sign of senile decay nor of a long delayed childhood, but rather a keen appreciation of the doings of the King's Boats."
- He achieved 1st class honours in Natural Sciences in 1901 - "The rejoicing of the school over Hodgkin's honours was intensified by a holiday, which was given in celebration of them."
- He assisted in a scientific survey of New Zealand's lakes in 1902.
- "Old Leightonians contemplating visiting Athens are advised not to throw stones at poodles. They may be dogs of high degree. The one whose repeated attacks George Hodgkin found it necessary to ward off with a stone, turned out to be the royal poodle; and it is understood that the police of Athens, scenting treason, arrested our generally law abiding representative on suspicion."
- He married Mary Fletcher Wilson in April 1913 at Friends' Meeting House, Bournville. They had three sons: Alan, Robin, and Keith.

The War
- He was an absolute conscientious objector. He would not take part in military service or any war work, as he, like many other Quakers, felt that to accept peaceful service for themselves was merely to force others to fight in their place.
- He died in hospital in Baghdad on the 24th of June 1916, of dysentery, on route to Armenia. An agent for the Lord Mayor's relief fund, it was his second expedition, the first took place in March 1916, to settle the allocation of funds and administer relief. The suffering of the Armenian people deeply affected George, and on his return he was dedicated to their cause, prepared to die in the effort of serving and supporting them.

A. H. Crossley

Full name: Alan Hastings Crossley
Years at L.P: 1893-1897
House: Grove
Date of birth: 15/06/1878
Higher education: Natural Sciences at Clare College Cambridge
Position in military: Lieutenant, 1st Hertfordshire Regiment
Date of death: 10/ 05/ 1917 (aged 39)
Reason for death: died of his wounds

At Leighton Park
- School Sport: 2nd XI football team plays forward on the Grove House team.
- Tennis: "Crossley's serving is at times very good, but is not sufficiently constant to win a victory from good opponents."
- Football 1897: "In the later matches, Crossley has improved very much as a back, doing the right thing, and exhibiting plenty of pluck."
- Crossley, GL Hodgkin, and H A Uprichard all played in the football team together.
- At the "Great Social" held in February 1887, after being postponed the previous term due to the measles, was a great success. Crossley was a steward, Hodgkin and Uprichard also participated.
- In 1897 Alan is awarded the annual prize for the best picture taken on the park for "A View of the Drive."

Post Leighton Park
- Natural Sciences at Clare College Cambridge, gained a second class in the Natural Science Tripos.
- "It is feared, since he did not put in an appearance at the summer meeting, that A H Crossley has lost himself in his rooms."
- "A H Crossley in the intervals of becoming a vegetarian, has passed his first exams, our congratulations are likewise due to him. At the same time, prompted by our excellent secretary, we would point out that the medical profession is sadly overcrowded, and that any OLs in the future thinking of

taking up this form of earning a livelihood, would do well to ask and take our Secretary's fatherly advice on the subject."

- "A H Crossley wishes it to be known that at present he does not see his way to become a vegetarian."
- He played for the OL football team.
- He was at St Thomas Hospital for 3 years after leaving the varsity, after which he did some research and other work at Crossley Sanatorium and later took to farming.
- "Alan Crossley is at T. & M. Dixons's model farm. They contract for milk free from tuberculosis for the Birmingham Hospital."
- He married in June 1911 and afterwards settled down to a country life with his wife Blanche at Old Letton Court, Hereford. He had a son Robert, born in 1912.
-

The War

- Second Lieutenant A H Crossley, 1st Herefordshire Regiment, died of wounds received in action at Gaza, in the Palestine Campaign, on the 19th April 1917 in hospital in Cairo.
- He is buried in the Cairo War Memorial Cemetery.

H.A. Uprichard

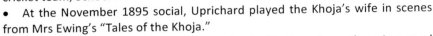

Full name: Henry Albert Uprichard
Years at L.P: 1893-1898
House: School
Position in military: Major, Royal Irish Rifles, 13th Battalion
Date of death: 01/07/1916 (aged 36)
Reason for death: machine-gun fire

At Leighton Park
- School Sport: 1st XI football team, 1st XI cricket team, School House football team
- At the November 1895 social, Uprichard played the Khoja's wife in scenes from Mrs Ewing's "Tales of the Khoja."
- Analysis of the boys football XI: Uprichard - "In this player there is a good deal of room for improvement: he is not yet a good shot, and has missed several easy goals this term, and his passes to the wings are bad: however he tries hard, and when he gets heavier will play a stronger game."
- The "Great Social" held in February 1887, HA Uprichard played a triangle in "The Toy Symphony."
- Football 1896: "Among the forwards, the play of the right wing has been the most pleasing feature; Uprichard on the outside running up and centring well, G Ll Hodgkin passing very accurately and pressing into goal, have between them been accountable for a very large percentage of our total score."
- Henry was awarded 2nd place in the photography competition for a photograph of Arborfield Church.
- At the Athletic Sports Day of April 1898, H A Uprichard broke the school long jump record with a jump of 18 foot 7½ inches. He also won kicking the football, came 2nd in the half mile race, the 1 mile race, and the "comic race."
- H A Uprichard, AH Crossley, and G Ll Hodgkin all played in the football team together.
- Cricket: "HA Uprichard has developed into a really good bat, with strokes all round the wicket. This is due in large measure to his constant and careful practice at the nets. He is a good field."

Post Leighton Park

- "OLs will hear with pride that HA Uprichard is among those who represent the North of Ireland at hockey. We hope his prowess, having brought him so far, will not stop here."

The War

- Major HA Uprichard was from County Down, Ireland. At Leighton Park he was a prominent athlete, and his interest in sport continued throughout his life. He was Master of the Iveagh Harriers, and played polo and hockey for the North of Ireland.
- On leaving school he entered the firm of Messrs Foster Green, of Belfast, and later he became its managing director.
- When war broke out he joined the Ulster Division of the Royal Irish Rifles as a Captain, getting his majority in 1916.
- He was killed by machine-gun fire while leading his battalion on Thiepval on July 1st 1916.
- His Commanding Officer writes: "His men worshipped him, as they were his first thought, and he could never do enough for them."

A.H. Richardson

Full name: Alfred Harold Richardson
Years at L.P: 1895-1901
House: Grove
Position in military: Corporal, 7th Battalion, Australian Imperial Force, Australian Infantry
Date of death: 08/04/1917
Reason for death: tuberculosis

At Leighton Park
- School Sport: 1st XI cricket team, 1st XI football team, Grove House swimming team, gymnastics
- Societies: The Secretary then President of the Senior Essay Society, Sub-Editor of *The Leightonian*, Debating Society
- At The Big Social 1897, Richardson did a display of leyden jars in the display of physical apparatus.
- "Richardson read an account of his "Impression of a Battle," the history of a battle he had seen in Rio de Janeiro." At the Show of Leisure work that year, the Union members acknowledged his essay was "quite the best we have known in the history of the union."
- At the Big Social of December 19th 1899: "The three scenes from *As You Like It* went very well. AH Richardson's Jaques, and A Warner's Orlando were perhaps the best parts."
- He was appointed prefect in September 1899.
- Analysis of the 1st XI cricket team 1900: "A useful field; his bowling which was good at the beginning of the season, has deteriorated; should cultivate a steadier style if he is to be of use. His batting is too wild."
- Athletic Sports Competition, Easter Monday 1901: AH Richardson came 1st in the hurdles race breaking the school record, 2nd in kicking the football, 100 yards, long jump, throwing the cricket ball, and putting the weight. Overall he came 2nd in the Challenge Cup.
- Football match report, LP vs Mansfield College, lost 4-0: "AH Richardson as usual played splendidly in goal; he saved many hard and difficult shots, thus preserving the team from a much greater defeat."
- Senior Essay Society: "AH Richardson contributed a paper, "The man who was born too early" in a light vein. This was an account of the origins of LP, in

which the author inclined to the view that all present were reincarnated cave men."

• "His contemporaries will recall his fine high jump of 5 feet, his brilliant fielding at point, and the prominent part he took in the Debating and Essay Societies. As a contributor to *The Leightonian* he was without a rival."

Post Leighton Park

• "AH Richardson at Queens College Oxford, having the happy history of the gentleman who confided to his audience the intelligence that he "was born a teetotaller," has safely experienced the disgusting ordeal of a "fresher's drunk.""

• "Harold Richardson has returned to England after six months tour in India. A book from his pen, entitled "Grandpa and Other Animals," will be published in the autumn."

• "Harold Richardson is for the moment busy in London interviewing publishers. He has recently been wandering in Russia and Switzerland."

The War

• Lance-Sergeant A Harold Richardson, 7th Battalion, A.I.F, Australian Infantry.

• Following a tour in Spain, he went home to Australia by way of the Siberian railway and Japan.

• Joining up early in the war, he was away from Australia for fifteen months, during most of which time he was laid low with enteric and rheumatic fever. After being in five different hospitals in England, he was sent home at the end of March, and died of tuberculosis when the ship was three days on the other side of Sierra Leone on the 8th of April 1917.

H. G. Barber

Full name: Herbert Graham Barber
Years at L.P: 1898-1902
House: School
Position in military: Captain, Hallamshire Rifles, 5th and 4th Battalion, York and Lancashire regiment.
Date of death: 07/07/1916 (aged 31)
Reason for death: killed in action

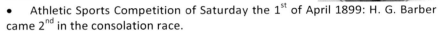

At Leighton Park

- School Sport: 1st XI football team, 2nd XI cricket team
- Athletic Sports Competition of Saturday the 1st of April 1899: H. G. Barber came 2nd in the consolation race.
- Match report 1900, L.P vs. Abingdon School: "The forwards' shooting was very bad, Warner's and Barber's in particular."
- He played the flute in the band.
- Analysis of the football team 1901: "H. G. Barber (left-outside) has become a success in his new position. Though without much pace he dribbles well, and has immensely improved his shooting, but his heading is weak. Always plays a hard working game."
- He came 2nd in the steeplechase on March 30th 1901.
- Analysis of the 2nd XI cricket 1901: "H. G. Barber (captain) – His batting has fallen off since the beginning of the term. He tries to bowl too fast, sacrificing pitch to pace. He has wasted his time at practicing too much."
- Athletic Sport Competition 1902: Barber came 1st in the steeplechase and the one mile race, breaking the school record; and 2nd in the half mile race, coming 2nd overall in the Godlee Cup.
- The Social Evening of February 1902: "In "A change of treatment" a nautical farce, H. G. Barber played a seamen. He also performed a flute solo."

Post Leighton Park

- He worked as a Director at Daniel Doncaster and Sons Steel Converters, Ltd., Sheffield.
- "The following rumour is indignantly denied – that H. G. Barber is undergoing treatment for "goggleyetus.""

The War

-      Captain H. Graham Barber, Hallamshire Rifles, 5th and 4th Battalion, York and Lancashire regiment, M.C, was from Sheffield. He left for France with the Hallamshires in April 1915. He was mentioned in Sir Douglas Haig's dispatches and was awarded the military cross. Major-General Percival, writes: "It would be almost impossible to speak too highly of him. He was an excellent officer in every respect, not only very gallant under fire, but a fine example to those under him at all times. Everything he had to do seems to have been well done. I have never had better reports on any officer than those sent to me by his Commanding Officer and by his Brigadier-General." Another officer wrote to Herbert's Father: "I perhaps, amongst those now left of the old Hallamshires, can best judge what a loss your son has been; not only to the country, but to our battalion in particular. During the war he brought out all the finest qualities of his nature, and from an easy-going and charming comrade, he became a most enthusiastic soldier and leader without sacrificing any of his charm-tug nature. He was always thinking of his men, and to me he appealed as one worthy of every help. I feel that I am not disclosing any secret when I say that his Colonel thought of him as his successor."

A. Warner

Full name: Archibald Warner
Years at L.P: 1899-1902
House: School
Higher education: Clare College Cambridge
Position in military: Second Lieutenant, 5th and 28th Battalion, London Regiment (Artist's Rifles)
Date of death: 01/07/1916 (aged 32)
Reason for death: hit by a shell

At Leighton Park
- School Sport: Captain of the 1st XI football team, Captain of the 1st XI cricket team, fives, athletics, gymnastics
- Societies: Junior and Senior Essay Society, played piano in the band, Sub-Editor of *The Leightonian*
- Football 1899: "Warner (left-inside) has improved, shoots rather weakly, and should learn to get control of the ball."
- At the Social Evening of April 1899 Archie played Falstaff in a dialogue from Shakespeare's *Henry IV*: "The dialogue from Henry IV seems to have lingered longest in the memory; the performers spoke out so well and enjoyed their parts so thoroughly that it was particularly pleasant to listen to."
- Match Report L.P vs. Reading School 1899, lost 12-1: "The school played up well, but the opponents goal was never in real danger with the exception of our one goal scored by Warner."
- Junior Essay Society: ""A day at Windsor" by A. Warner was a graphic description of how a party from Leighton Park had spent their exeat."
- In the fives tournament of 1901, Warner came 2nd after losing to Braithwaite in the final.
- Archie was appointed prefect in May 1901.
- Football 1902: "A. Warner has proved an excellent captain. Indeed it is not too much to say that the success of the season is in a great measure due to his untiring efforts."
- Analysis of the 1st XI cricket team: "A. Warner (captain) has kept wicket very much better this season; has improved his batting, but is still too stiff to allow him to score freely."
-

Post Leighton Park

- Cambridge rowing letter: "At the beginning of the term A. Warner was often observed tubbing (coaching) *particularly* unpromising freshers. "That's the worst of being *such* a good coach," he explainedArchie was appointed to captain the O.L football team in 1903.
- "We congratulate A. Warner on being a qualified solicitor."
- "A. Warner has been seen several times during the summer in an out-of-the-way place in Ireland sitting on the carrier of a motor bicycle revelling in great speeds. He likes it so much that he has dreams of giving up captaincy of the Reigate Priory F.C and taking to the open road."
- At the O.L dinner in 1913, A. Warner made a toast to the "ladies" of the school, recalling the interest they always displayed in the boy's health and activities.
- He married Norah Goodbody in August 1914 at Friends Meeting House.

The War

- Second Lieutenant Archibald Warner was from Croydon. He obtained a commission in the London Rifle Brigade, and had only been in France a few weeks, when he fell. Early in the attack on July 1st a big shell came through the parapet of an advanced British trench and killed him by its concussion. He showed great optimism and cheery confidence while at the Front, and used to go out into No Man's Land when necessary, as though he were looking at the flowers in his own garden.

C. H. Thorpe

Full name: Clive Halliburton Thorpe
Years at LP: 1901-1903
House: Grove
Position in military: Company Quartermaster Sergeant, C Squadron, West Kent Yeomanry
Date of death: 08/11/1918 (aged 32)
Reason for death: hit by a shell

At Leighton Park
- He was a member of the Natural History Society.
- At the Social Evening of December 1902, in a performance of "Dormitory scene" Thorpe played a prefect.
- At the Mid-Term Social the same year, Thorpe was part of a trio that sang "Harmonious Blacksmith" by Handel and "Huntsmen's Chorus" by Weber.
- He played a surgeon in "A French Duel" by Mark Twain at the Easter Social in 1903.

Post Leighton Park
- "C H Thorpe has joined the army, and is a Sergeant in the West Kent Yeomanry."

The War
- The last week of war, 8th of November 1918 claimed Clive H Thorpe who was killed by a shell as the British troops were entering Tournai, Belgium.
- He went through the campaigns of Gallipoli and Palestine before serving on the Western Front and was mentioned in Sir Douglas Haig's Despatches; all this time he retained his post as Company Quartermaster Sergeant, declining to take any steps towards a Commission. He preferred to remain with his chums of the West Kent Yeomanry, and to continue the work he knew. He is buried in the Belgian Cemetery at Tournai.

A S Lloyd

Full name: Alan Scrivener Lloyd
Years at LP: 1901-1907
House: Grove
Higher education: Trinity College Cambridge
Position in military: Lieutenant, "C" battery, 78th
Brigade, Royal Field Artillery
Date of death: 04/08/1916 (aged 27)
Reason for death: hit by a shell

At Leighton Park

- School Sport: Captain of 1st XI cricket team for three years, 1st XI football team, Grove tennis team.
- Societies: President of Debating Society, Secretary of Essay Society, Sub-Editor of *The Leightonian*
- At the Big Social in 1901, A S Lloyd played Alice in "The Mock Turtles Story." A year later he reprised his role as Alice: "AS Lloyd reappeared in an old part, which must by this time have become a second nature, which he finds it hard to put off."
- Debating Society: In a debate entitled "The new motor bill imposes unreasonable restrictions on motoring" "AS Lloyd, in opposing, made a characteristic and lively speech, but showed considerable ignorance of the facts of the case."
- Essay: ""Wee Macgregor's double" was a very clever story written by A Lloyd, describing his supposed experiences with fellow passengers in a railway carriage, at the age of 63."
- "AS Lloyd is the captain of the boys 1st XI cricket team, a post of honour which he has satisfactorily filled."
- He was appointed prefect in September 1905.
- He was unanimously voted President of the Debating Society.
- In the Athletic Sports Competition 1907, A S Lloyd came 1st in the 100 yards race in a time of 11 seconds.
- "We heartily congratulate AS Lloyd on his fine batting display against the OLs. He is the first boy who has scored a century for a number of years; in fact we can find no record of another, though rumours speak of one who did it "in the great days of old". The athletic committee have given Lloyd a bat and will treat future "centuries" in a similar manner."

Post Leighton Park

• "AS Lloyd has created quite a sensation at Trinity this term, he has had no less than three different motorbikes in the course of a few weeks, and his dog is as much talked about. He may occasionally be found playing golf, having recently created the unique record of losing ten balls in nine holes."

• He went on the 1909 OL cricket tour with Warner and Lennard.

• On going up to Cambridge, he took up rowing.

• "Congratulations to Alan Lloyd on being in the winning boat in the Coxswainless Fours. First Trinity were a phenomenally heavy crew, averaging 12 stone 13 lb."

• Having taken his degree in Economics and Agriculture, he studied farming in Yorkshire and Scotland. He then visited the Argentine and South Africa, and indulged in some big game shooting in North West Rhodesia.

• "A S Lloyd and his brother took a motor trip to the Pyrenees at Christmas time. We hear that they averaged 140 miles a day, had 15 punctures, and ruined 4 new tyres. For further details apply to either or both, as their accounts differ wildly."

• "Alan Lloyd is studying the breeding of shorthorn cattle on the Earl of Moray's estate in Perthshire. His recreation is deerstalking, but crawl as he may, he cannot conceal himself."

• He married Dorothy Margaret Hewetson, and they had a son in 1915.

The War

• Lieutenant Lloyd received his commission in the Royal Field Artillery in September 1914, and after eight months training in Dorset, his Brigade went to the Front.

• When he fell, on 04/08/1916, he was on night duty as observation officer for his Battery. He was struck by a direct shell while repairing the telephone wire, death being almost instantaneous. His fellow officers write that he was brave and fearless, but not reckless.

• He was awarded the Military Cross.

• He was buried a few miles behind the trenches in Dartmoor Cemetery, Becordel-Becourt, some of his men walking five miles in order to be present. He left a widow and an infant son.

F. H. G. Wallis

Full name: Francis Herbert Guy Wallis
Years at L.P: 1902-1906
House: School
Position in military: Captain, East Yorkshire Regiment, 11th Battalion
Date of death: 17/05/1918 (aged 28)
Reason for death: killed in action

At Leighton Park

- School Sport: 1st XI football team, Captain of 2nd XI cricket team
- Societies: Secretary of Junior Essay Society, Debating Society
- Analysis of the 2nd XI football team: "G. Wallis has been a very successful centre forward. He passes well, and although rather slow at times, he is distinctly dangerous in front of goal."
- He made the only century of the 1905 cricket season, in a 2nd XI match against Clayesmore School.
- At the Social Evening of December 1902, F. H. G. Wallis made a waxwork of Tweedledum and Tweedledee with A. Wallis.
- Junior Essay Society: F. H. G. Wallis read an essay on "Basing Castle" near Basingstoke.
- Junior Athletics Competition 1904: F. H .G. Wallis came 2nd in kicking the football and the hurdle race.
- Social Evening 1905: G. Wallis played Borachio, and N. M. Angus played Sexton in scenes from Shakespeare's *Much Ado About Nothing*.
- Junior Essay Society: "G. Wallis, who has been secretary for the last 12 months, resigned his post, and R. Ashby was appointed in his place."
- The Big Social 1906: At the exhibition of leisure work, F. H. G. Wallis won 1st prize for machine construction. He also took part in a gymnastics display with A. S. Lloyd and W. B. Vickers, and reprised his role as Borachio in *Much Ado About Nothing* with N. M. Angus.
- In The Life Saving Society examination, Wallis was awarded Medallion.

Post Leighton Park

- He worked at Wallis and Stevensons Ltd. (Engineers)
- Hobbies: motoring, shooting, fishing and winter sports in Switzerland.

The War

- Captain Guy Wallis, was from Basingstoke. On leaving school he entered the firm of Messrs. Wallis and Stevens, Ltd., with which he was connected for eight years. At the outbreak of war he was one of the first to join the Colours. Commencing in the officers' training corps at Epsom, he was soon drafted to Hull and gazetted 2nd-Lieutenant, 11th East Yorks in September 1914, Lieutenant in November 1914, and subsequently, after much active service, Captain in November 1916. He was on active service in Egypt on the Canal Defences and Desert Patrols (Sinai Peninsula). Recalled to France in March 1916, he at once commenced duties in the trenches. He was in the battle of the Somme on July 1st 1916, and again on November 13th at the battle of the Ancre. After twelve months' active service in France he was invalided to England in 1917. On discharge from Queen Alexandra's Hospital at Millbank, he resumed duty at Withernsea. April the 6th 1918 saw him in France once more, and from the 9th to the 14th he took part in the magnificent defence by the 31st Division. Continuing his duties at the front, he wrote on May 15th—" In an hour's time we take over the front line again. My Company goes first." News of his death reached his home on May 18th.

W. B. Vickers

Full name: William Burnell Vickers
Years at L.P: 1903-1908
House: School
Position in military: "D" company, 3rd and 21st
service Battalions (Public Schools Battalion)
Royal Fusiliers. Then Royal Garrison Artillery,
184th Siege Battery.
Date of death: 21/06/1917 (aged 26)
Reason for death: killed in action

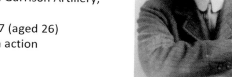

At Leighton Park

- Societies: Secretary of the Camera Club, Natural History Society, played second violin in the band.
- At the Mid-Term Social on November 12th 1903, W. B. Vickers sang "Who is Sylvia?" by Schubert.
- Athletic Sport Competition 1905: In junior events, W. B. Vickers came 1st in kicking the football, breaking the school record with a distance of 51 yards. He also came 1st in the 100 yards race and long jump, and 2nd in throwing the cricket ball, the quarter mile, and the 220 yards race.
- Aquatic Sports Competition 1905: Junior events – W. B. Vickers came 1st in one length, and one length on back.
- At the Big Social 1906, W. B. Vickers won prizes for photography, lantern slides, and physical apparatus. He also took part in a gymnastics display with A. S. Lloyd and F. H. G. Wallis, and played second violin in the band.
- End of Term Social December 1906: "Barry Pain's dialogue "Shopping" was well acted by N. M. Angus and W. B. Vickers."
- He was appointed prefect in September 1907.
- He played in the 2nd XI football team with Angus, Barlow and Ashby.
- At the 1907 exhibition of leisure work, W. B. Vickers won 3 prizes in photography, 1st prize for both enlargement and ordinary prints, and 2nd prize in lantern slides. He also won 1st prize in music for violin, and scientific apparatus for his harmonograph. Overall, he won the most 1st prizes.
- At the End of Term Social in 1908, W. B. Vickers contributed a Minuet by Handel as a farewell violin solo.

Post Leighton Park
- W. B. Vickers spends his spare time yachting on the Trent and is in his happiest frame of mind when "the lee scuppers are awash and the cabin is a bath."
- W. B. Vickers on his Rudge motorcycle came 1st in one of the events of the Nottingham and District Motorcycle Club Amber Hill-Climbing Competition.

The War
- Second Lieutenant W. B. Vickers, who was killed on June 21st 1917, was from Nottingham. At the outbreak of the war he was in Norway, and when he returned he enlisted in the Public Schools Battalion of the Royal Fusiliers. He obtained his commission in the regiment in March 1915 with school friend E. W. Lennard, and went to the Front in the following November. He returned home in July 1916, having been transferred to the Garrison Artillery, but went abroad again with a Siege Battery last October. Major A. 0. Ellis, Royal Garrison Artillery, wrote to Vickers' parents: "Your son was the most loyal comrade I have ever had. I have never known an officer more beloved by his men; he had the wonderful gift of true sympathy, so that all, including myself, would go to him with their troubles and difficulties. He was always thinking of others, and in his last letter he asked me not to say anything when writing to you that would be likely to cause you any anxiety on his account."

N. M. Angus

Full name: Norman Mortimer Angus
Years at Leighton Park: 1904–1907
House: School
Date of birth: 30/04/1890
Position in military: Private, 7th Battalion, The Buffs (East Kent Regiment)
Date of death: 03/05/1917
Reason for death: killed in action

At Leighton Park

- Sport: 2nd XI football team, 2nd XI cricket team, tennis
- Societies: Debating Society, Essay Society, Secretary of Literary Historical and Archaeological Society, Natural History
- Junior Essay Society 1905: "A good description of the Crystal Palace was read by N. Angus, who had spent an enjoyable day there."
- Social Evening 1905: G. Wallis played Borachio, and N. M. Angus played Sexton in scenes from Shakespeare's *Much Ado About Nothing*.
- The best of seven essays at the Junior Essay Reading: "The Autobiography of a Wren.""
- At the Big Social 1906, in the exhibition of leisure work won prizes for junior essay, elocution, recitation and reading.
- End of Term Social 1906: In scenes from the life of Richard I, G. Wallis played the King, and N. Angus played Queen Berengaria.
- He played in the 2nd XI football team
- End of Term Social December 18th 1906: "Barry Pain's dialogue "Shopping" was well acted by N. M. Angus and W. B. Vickers."

Post Leighton Park

- He worked as a bank clerk in Cardiff.

The War

- Private Norman M. Angus, 7th Battalion, The Buffs (East Kent Regiment) was from Aberystwyth.. In the early months of the war, he offered himself for military service, but the bank kept him back as indispensable till April 1916 when he joined the Bankers' Battalion of the East Kent Regiment, and after six months training in Kent, went out to France in November 1916. His first experience of fighting in the open was on May 3rd 1917, when his regiment took part in an advance through the village of Cherisy, which ended in a disastrous retreat. He, with four-fifths of his platoon was reported missing. His fate was for a long time uncertain, but after nearly twelve months, definite evidence came to hand that he had fallen. All who knew him will agree that he was little suited for a soldier's life, but he faced its hardships and dangers cheerfully, and without complaint. The experience seemed to have the effect on him that it had on so many, that of deepening the sense of the value and interest of life and the possibilities of the future. In a letter written on his 27th birthday, a few days before he fell, he expresses his anticipation that he will return after the war to take a share in the work of reconstruction, and to make more out of life than he had done in the past. He had indeed always shown a practical interest in social and religious work, and had taken an active part in such work in Cardiff. Wherever he went, he won confidence and affection by his gentle courtesy, his cheery good humour, his transparent sincerity and his readiness to help.

R. Ashby

Full name: Raymond Ashby
Years at Leighton Park: 1905-1907
House: School
Position in military: DMC (distinguished military cross) Lance Corporal Ashby, 8th Battalion, Royal Fusiliers
Date of death: 07/10/1916 (aged 25)
Reason for death: killed at the Somme

At Leighton Park

- School Sport: Captain of the 2nd XI football team
- Societies: secretary of the Junior Essay Society.
- At the Athletic Sports Competition on Saturday 8th April, R. Ashby came 1st in high jump, and 2nd in half mile.
- The Big Social 1906: At the exhibition of leisure work, Ashby won 1st prize for Junior Essay.
- He replaced F. H. G. Wallis as the secretary for the Junior Essay Society.
- He played in the 2nd XI football team with Vickers, Barlow and Angus.
- Analysis of the 2nd XI football team: "Ashby has worked very hard at centre-half. He has made a keen and enthusiastic captain."
- "The pick of this term's essays so far have been, R. Ashby's on 'The Founding of the British Empire,' which was a really good paper, and a most interesting subject."

The War

- Lance Corporal Raymond Ashby joined the Public Schools Battalion, Royal Fusiliers in March 1916 as a private of choice. He went out as a volunteer to France in July, and was then moved into the 8th Battalion. At Poziers he was wounded in four places in an attack, but still managed to capture 20-30 German Prisoners. He was not long in hospital, and his General soon after gave him an ornamental card of honour for his gallantry. He was now made Lance Corporal, but was soon given Sergeant's work and very heavy responsibility and command. In September he was awarded the DMC; the whole Battalion was pleased and proud of him, cheering him when it was announced. Raymond was then in another terrible advance on October 7th 1916, near Le Transloy and Flers. It was against fearful odds, and his battalion was almost completely annihilated; he was leading his platoon in the centre of attack and was hit when not far from our lines, and was seen to fall wounded by two of his comrades, one of whom tried in vain to find him when he was able to return the spot at night. The war office reported his as "Missing" and no more reliable news of him has been heard since. Letters from the men of his section show how much he was beloved by them; they say he was kindness itself, and his one thought seemed to be how he could make their lot less hard; they were proud to be under him. His captain too expressed much regret at his loss, and great appreciation of him as a "conspicuously brave man" reliable at all times, and most efficient and valuable in "dangerous and trying" patrol and reconnaissance night work, on account of his thorough knowledge of German and French.

F. W. Knott

Full name: Fredrick William Knott
Years at Leighton Park: 1905-1909
House: Grove
Date of birth: 04/03/1892
Position in military: Second Lieutenant, 9th Battalion, Yorkshire Regiment.
Date of death: 07/06/1917 (aged 25)
Reason for death: hit by a shell

At Leighton Park

- School Sport: Captain of the 2nd XI football team
- Societies: Secretary of Literary Historical and Archaeological Society, Natural History Society, Essay Society, Camera club, Debating society
- Analysis of the 2nd XI football team: "Knott (captain) plays hard at centre-half, making great use of his head."
- He played in the 2nd XI football team with Morton, Barlow and E. Lennard.
- The Big Social 1906: F. W. Knott read the part of Mother Jaguar in a recitation of Kipling's "Just So" Stories.
- Junior Essay Society: "F. W. Knott described to us "A Day in Switzerland," that he had spent near the picturesque village of Zermatt.
- At the musical society's 11th Annual Musical Evening on July 31st 1906, Knott played a violin solo - "Knott produced a very good tone in his violin solo."
- Aquatic Sports Competition 1907: "Amongst the juniors, Knott proved to be the best swimmer." In the junior events he came 1st in four lengths and one length, and 3rd in diving, one length on the back, and plunge.
- At the 1907 exhibition of leisure work, F. W. Knott won 1st prize for junior essay.
- Gymnastics Competition 1908: F. W. Knott came 4th in parallel bars.
- In The Life Saving Society examination, Knott was awarded Medallion.
- "F. W. Knott, at left-half has played several matches, he passes straight and uses his head whenever possible."
- At the Big Social of December 1908 he did a chemistry demonstration of "singing flames."

Post Leighton Park
- He was an apprentice at the Bessbrook (Northern Ireland) Spinning Company.
- He played for the Bessbrook Tennis Club.
- "Hobbies: Singing, motorcycling, (smoking)"
- "Married? Not Yet!"

The War
- Second Lieutenant F. W. Knott, Yorkshire Regiment; killed by a shell on the 7th of June 1917, was from Wilmslow, Manchester. Before completing his apprenticeship he was offered the post of secretary to the Company, which employs over two thousand workpeople. Lieutenant Knott left the firm in October 1915, and volunteered for service. He joined the Inns of Court Officers' Training Corps, and, after training, received his commission in the Yorkshires in May 1916, and was promoted to Lieutenant for bombing instruction in September. He went to France in March. The officer commanding his battalion in a letter to his parents wrote: "It is with the very deepest sympathy of all the officers of the battalion that I write to inform you that your son was killed instantly by a shell during the battle on the morning of the 7th of July. He was a brave and noble fellow, beloved of all his men, to whom he always set a fine example of courage and devotion to duty. I shall feel his loss keenly, as he had endeared himself to me during the all too short time he was with us.

M. S. Wills

Full name: Michael Seccombe Wills
Years at Leighton Park: 1906-1908
House: School
Position in military: Sergeant, 6th Battalion, Somerset Light Infantry
Date of death: 12/08/1915 (aged 21)
Reason for death: killed in action

At Leighton Park
- M. S. Wills was a member of the Natural History Society.

Post Leighton Park
- Went to Blundell's School in Devon.
- He worked at The Imperial Tobacco Company in Bristol.

The War
- M. S. Wills was at Leighton Park from May 1906 to April 1908. He then went to Blundell's where he joined the Officers' Training Corps. On completing his education he took up a clerical appointment with the Imperial Tobacco Company, Bristol. On the outbreak of war he was amongst the first of the staff to enlist. Rejecting a commission, he preferred to serve in the ranks with his companions, and joined the 6th Somersets, a "pals" Battalion. He soon became a Sergeant and left for Flanders on 21st of May. He was mortally wounded in one of the battles in August. He was the first O.L to fall in battle.

G. A. Howkins

Full name: George Addington Howkins
Years at Leighton Park: 1906-1908
House: Grove
Higher education: Trinity College Cambridge
Position in military: Second Lieutenant, 12th
Battalion, Northumberland Fusiliers, Machine Gun
Section
Date of death: 25/09/1915
Reason for death: killed in action

At Leighton Park
- He joined Leighton Park in May 1906, from Wokingham.
- At the 11th Annual Musical Evening on July 31st 1906, G. A. Howkins recited "Father William" by Lewis Carroll.
- Mid Term Social 1907: He took part in an 'Uncle Tom's Cabin' scene.
- He was a member of the Natural History Society.
- At the 1907 exhibition of leisure work, G. A. Howkins won 1st prize for his birds' eggs collection.

Post Leighton Park
- He went to Harrow, and then on to Cambridge.

The War
- G. A. Howkins, 2nd Lieutenant, 12th Battalion, Northumberland Fusiliers, Machine Gun Section, was killed in action in France on 25th of September. On the outbreak of the war he was gazetted to the 12th Northumberland Fusiliers.

H. C. Barlow

Full name: Harold Carver Barlow
Years at Leighton Park: 1906-1909
House: School
Date of birth: 29/08/1891
Position in military: Lieutenant, Manchester Regiment, 9th Squadron and 20th Battalion, Lancashire Fusiliers, Royal Flying Corps
Date of death: 18/06/1917 (aged 25)
Reason for death: his plane was shot down

At Leighton Park

- School Sport: 1st and 2nd XI football teams, cricket, tennis, fives
- Societies: Junior Essay, Debating Society, Literary Historical and Archaeological Society
- Analysis of the 2nd XI football team: "Barlow, though small, should make an excellent back."
- He played in the 2nd XI football team with Vickers, Angus and Ashby.
- Junior Essay Society: Barlow read "The siege of Stirling Castle."
- Football 1908: "Barlow is a very promising half-back, and would have played regularly in the boys 1st XI, if the team had had their proper number of matches."
- "We congratulate H. C. Barlow on winning the fives championship, but regret that the competition was so poor."
- Football 1908-1909: "H. C. Barlow (centre or right-half) Rather slow in tackling but passes well to his forwards; takes corners nicely; should learn to use his head far more, especially when playing at centre-half; is apt to kick too hard."
- Cricket 1909: "H. C. Barlow – An excellent all round player. A very good bat, with strong defence and good hitting power. Scored a fine century against Newbury School, and another under somewhat unsatisfactory conditions in a second innings against Reading Wednesday. A useful bowler and a very fine field." He was awarded a bat for his centuries.
- He won the 1909 tennis tournament.
- In The Life Saving Society examination, Barlow was awarded Medallion.

Post Leighton Park

- "H. C. Barlow is working for his father's business in Manchester. For recreation he plays lacrosse for Marple."
- "H. C. Barlow has taken up lacrosse and singing as hobbies."
- "H. C. Barlow and his sister won the open mixed doubles at the Malvern Tennis Tournament at Whitsuntide."

The War

- H. C. Barlow was originally with a Lancashire Bantam Regiment (Bantam: A Battalion of men shorter than the army's minimum regulation height)
- In February 1917, a request to transfer to the Royal Flying Corps was granted and he joined 9th Squadron as an observer. At 11am on 18 June, Lieutenant Reginald W Ellis took off with Harold as his observer on a photographic reconnaissance mission. Their plane was an RE8, numbered A4290.

Reports suggest their plane was shot down by Manfred von Richthofen, the famous "Red Baron" North of Ypres. The plane had crashed on the German side of the front line and Harold was originally posted as being missing. Reports reached home stating that he had not been injured and had been taken prisoner. The reports were mistaken and both men had died. They were buried by the Germans. The verification of his death took several months to come through.

J. S. Inglis

Full name: Arthur James Stephen Inglis
Years at Leighton: 1906-1911
House: Grove
Position in military: in training
Date of death: 13/12/1915 (aged 23)
Reason for death: motorcycle accident

At Leighton Park

- School Sport: football, cricket, tennis
- Societies: Debating, Natural History, LHA
- At the Big Social of December 1908, he played
the Ghost of Jacob Marley in scenes from Charles Dickens' *Christmas Carol*.
- Football 1909: "A. J. Inglis (right-back) – Kicks well, but does not make enough out of his pace. Might be more robust."
- Inglis, Keep and Brain played for the Grove House football team.
- He won the 1910 steeplechase, despite the fact "a strong wind impeded competitors."
- "Criticism of the cricket team: Inglis - A useful change bowler on his day. His batting has much improved. A fair fielder."
- At the Aquatic Sports Competition 1910, he came first place in all the open events, thus winning the Lister Harrison Cup.

Post Leighton Park

- "Inglis is working in a chartered accountants office in Glasgow."
- Hobbies: photography, fretwork

The War

- It is with deep regret that we record the death of A. J. S. Inglis. He was motorcycling, when something went wrong with the engine, and he collided with a telegraph pole. He never regained consciousness. On leaving Leighton Park, he entered his father's business for a time; but recently became a pupil of an aircraft school in the Lake District, with the object of serving his country as soon as he was qualified. Those who were at school with him will remember his plucky running and his ability in taking a humorous part in plays. Himself always bright and happy, he had the power of passing these virtues to those with whom he came in contact.

J. M. Downie

Full name: James Maitland Downie
Years at Leighton Park: 1906-1911
House: School
Date of birth: 30/05/1893
Higher education: Christ's College Cambridge
Position in military: Captain, Royal Army
Medical Corps
Date of death: 28/10/1918 (aged 25)
Reason for death: pneumonia

At Leighton Park

- Societies: Literary Historical and Archaeological Society, secretary of Natural History Society, secretary of Junior Essay Society, piano in band, Debating Society, Camera Club
- At the Big Social of December 1908 he took part in a gymnastics display with E. W. Lennard, played a piano solo, and took part in a scotch dance with J. Farmer.
- Junior Essay: He read an essay "A Practical Joke."
- End of Term Social 1908: "J. M. Downie and Keen gave us "Pomp and Circumstance" arranged as a piano duet. We must not forget, too, the appearance of Downie in his tartans."
- Gymnastics Competition of the 17th of November 1908: Downie came 2nd in boom, horizontal bars, ropes and horse.
- .
- Debating Society: "J. M. Downie, in a strong maiden speech, condemned the immense lines on which modern advertising is carried on."
- At the 1910 exhibition of leisure work, Downie won a special prize for a study of bird skulls with an accompanying illustrated catalogue. He was also awarded 3rd prize for piano, 1st prize for concerted music, and 1st prize for recitation.

Post Leighton Park

- Cambridge University, medical student taking Natural Sciences.
- He contributed a song in the O.L Dinner of April 1913.
- Hobbies: natural history, fishing, philosophy, walking, music (vocal and instrumental), croquet, golf and tennis

- "Married? Nay!"
- "J. M. Downie has not reappeared on the river this year. He finds that the claims of his corpse, and an occasional game of golf, fill up his afternoons."
- He was awarded a Bachelor Scholarship in 1914.

The War

- Captain J. Maitland Downie, R.A.M.C, died of pneumonia, following influenza, on the 28th of October 1918, at Basra, Mesopotamia. Since Christmas, 1917, he had been O.C. of a hospital at Qualet Saleh, on the Tigris, where his work lay greatly among the Arabs. He had the faculty of making the most of his surroundings and of getting enjoyment from the country, the people and the language. He was such a lover of children and of nature; his pets in Mesopotamia included a wild cat and an owl. For his latest post he had to pass an exam in Arabic and had recently also learnt Persian and had applied to be transferred to Persia. By those, who knew him, few men will be more missed.

J. S. Morton

Full name: J. S. Morton
Years at LEIGHTON PARK: 1907-1908
House: School
Date of birth: 15/04/1892
Position in military: Corporal, 15th Battalion, West Yorkshire Regiment
Date of death: 01/07/1916 (aged 24)
Reason for death: killed in action

At Leighton Park
- He joined Leighton Park in 1907 from Leeds.
- He played in the 2nd XI football team, with Knott, Barlow and E. W. Lennard.

Post Leighton Park
- "J. S. Morton after 18 months experience in Glasgow has returned to Leeds, where he is helping to manage his father's cloth factory."

The War
- He went out to Egypt, and later was transferred to the Western Front. He was killed during the first advance while rushing the German trenches on the 1st of July 1916.

J. Farmer

Full name: James Farmer
Years at Leighton Park: 1907-1909
House: School
Position in military: Canadian Contingent
Date of death: 1916
Reason for death: killed in action

At Leighton Park
- He joined LEIGHTON PARK in 1907 from Glasgow.
- Societies: Junior Essay Society, Natural History Society
- At the Big Social of December 1908, he took part in a scotch dance with J. M. Downie - "Four kilted Scotchmen gave us a delightful exhibition of their national sword dance."
- Aquatic Sports Competition 1908: J. Farmer came 2nd in one length on back.

Post Leighton Park
- J. Farmer is a homesteader (lives self-sufficiently) at Viking in Canada.

The War
- James Farmer was the son of Mr J. Farmer of Parkhead Cross, Glasgow. On leaving school, he went to Canada, returning to England to join the Canadian contingent.

E W Lennard

Full name: Edward Wood Lennard
Years at Leighton Park: 1907-1909
House: Grove
Position in military: 3rd Battalion (Public Schools
Battalion) Royal Fusiliers.
Second Lieutenant, Royal Irish Rifles
Date of death: 30/11/1917 (aged 28)
Reason for death: killed in action

At Leighton Park

- School Sport: 1st XI football team, cricket, tennis
- Societies: Camera Club, Debating Society, Essay Society
- He was appointed prefect in September 1907.
- He won the Championship at the 1908 Aquatic Sports Contest.
- Analysis of the football 1st XI: "Lennard (centre half), a good tackler who uses his weight and his head to great advantage."
- At the "Big Social" of December 1908 he played The Ghost of Christmas Past in scenes from Charles Dickens' *Christmas Carol.*
- At the 1909 exhibition of leisure work he won 1st prize for coins.
- He played on the Grove House tennis team with A S Lloyd.
- Cricket 1908: "EW Lennard – Bats with much power and in excellent style; his century against Bedales was a treat to witness; bowls well; a safe catch and good field."
- At the Gymnastics Competition in 1908, Lennard came 2nd overall in the Fry Shield.

Post Leighton Park

- He took part in the 1909 OL cricket tour with Lloyd and Warner.
- "EW Lennard on his motorcycle took first place in the Leicester and District hill-climbing Contest."

The War

- Second Lieutenant EW Lennard was from Leicester. His contemporaries will not forget his style as a cricketer, and his keen interest in the Essay and Debating Societies. On leaving, he entered his grandfather's business.
- Joining up, he served in the ranks for some time with school friend W B Vickers, and later held a commission in the 5th Royal Irish Rifles.

- Killed in action on 30th November 1917
- He is remembered on the Tyne Cot Memorial (Panel 138 to 140 and 162 to 162A and 163A).
- He left a widow Annie Eliza

A.E. Mitchell

Full name: A. Eric Mitchell
Years at Leighton Park: 1907-1912
House: School
Position in military: Corporal, Northumberland Fusiliers
Date of death: 09/04/1917 (aged 22)
Reason for death: shot by a sniper

At Leighton Park
- Societies: Natural History Society, Literary Historical and Archaeological Society, Essay Society
- At the "Big Social" of December 1908 he played Tiny Tim in scenes from Charles Dickens' *Christmas Carol*.
- Junior Essay Society: "A. E. Mitchell read a descriptive essay on "A Yorkshire Dale and its surroundings.""
- He was appointed prefect in September 1912.
- Senior Essay: He read an essay on 'The Chinese Empire.'

Post Leighton Park
- "He is taking a textiles course at Leeds University."

The War
- From Egypt, the regiment was sent to France and took part in the battle of the Somme. In this battle Mitchell was wounded, and spent a month in hospital. On recovery he was transferred to the Northumberland Fusiliers. He was shot by a sniper on Easter Monday 1917 whilst gallantly leading his platoon. An officer wrote: "We shall all miss him very much, because he was liked by everyone in the Company, his very cheerful disposition being a great boon to us in the very trying circumstances which we had to undergo."

D. S. H. Keep

Full name: Douglas Scrivener Howard Keep
Years at LP: 1907-1912
House: Grove
Higher education: Wadham College Oxford
Position in military: Captain, 7th Battalion, Bedfordshire Regiment
Date of death: 14/07/1917 (aged 24)
Reason for death: hit by a shell

At Leighton Park

- School Sport: 1st XI football team
- Societies: L.H.A, Essay Society, Debating Society, Camera Club
- Junior Essay Society: "DSH Keep dealt with "Sponges and the methods of gathering and preparing them.""
- Debating Society: Keep proposed the motion "Modern sports and pastimes are becoming less manly."
- He played on the Grove football team with Inglis and Brain.
- Analysis of the football team: Keep – A steady methodical right half. Should practice increased speed in running and turning. Does not always keep sufficiently near his forwards."
- He was appointed prefect in January 1911.
- At the 1912 exhibition of leisure work, Keep won 1st prize for prose essay.

The War

- Captain DSH Keep was in the midst of his course at Oxford when war broke out. Obtaining a commission, he ultimately gained the rank of Captain.
- Awarded the Military Cross in September 1916: "For conspicuous gallantry in action. He organised and led repeated bombing attacks on the enemy strong points. On one occasion, with only three men and no bombs, he remained in close proximity to the enemy for one and a half hours."

Awarded the Royal Humane Society's Medal for life-saving

Having survived 1st July 1916, the Svwaben Redoubt assaults, Ancre operations and Arras battles, he was killed by a shell as his party were burying cables near Ypres.

His body was recovered and he was buried with full military honours at Reninghelst New Military Cemetery, Belgium (Grave III F26)

- His Padre wrote: "The greatness of his nature was revealed to me by the wonderful sense of responsibility he had for his men. If they fell, it really hurt him, and busy as he was, he never neglected to unite the friends of a single man. His achievements and influences will never be lost as long as this battalion remains, and then it will live on in scores of simple homes and hearts."

- He left a widow Agnes Rosa.

F. S. Brain

Full name: Francis Sydney Brain
Years at Leighton Park: 1908-1912
House: Grove
Date of birth: 22/12/1893
Higher education: Law at Trinity College
Cambridge
Position in military: Second Lieutenant, 9th
Battalion, Royal Berkshire Regiment
Date of death: 03/10/1918 (aged 24)
Reason for death: hit by a shell

At Leighton Park
- School Sport: 1st XI football team, 1st XI cricket team
- Societies: Secretary of the Debating Society, Essay Society, Literary Historical and Archaeological Society, Musical Society, sub-editor of *The Leightonian*
- At the Big Social of December 1908, he did a chemistry demonstration of "Geissler tubes."
- At the 1910 exhibition of leisure work he won 1st prize for piano and concerted music.
- Essay Society: read an essay on "Homer and his works."
- Analysis of the 1st XI football team 1910: "Brain plays hard, but is not very sure, sometimes centring rather wildly."
- He was appointed prefect in September 1911.
- He was awarded the O.L scholarship in April 1913.
- He gained an Open Scholarship for intending students in law at Trinity College Cambridge 1913: "We have every confidence that he will be a credit to his old school."

Post Leighton Park
- "Brain no longer keeps a piano in his rooms. Though this may add to his legal studies, it has deprived his room of its old charm. He is in great demand in many other places where pianos are to be found. "
- "F. S. Brain may be seen any afternoon rowing four in a Hall crock. On one occasion his boat varied the afternoon's work with a bathe. We consider it tactful not to enquire whether this was voluntary."

- "F. S. Brain, not content with his honours achieved in the soccer line, has taken to rowing again this term and was in the hall boat that made three bumps. Congratulations on getting a first in his law mays last December"
- He got engaged to Miss Muriel Ryan.

The War
- After joining the Cambridge Officers' Training Corps, he was gazetted in 1915 to the Royal Berks Regiment, but for the whole two years that he was in France, he was attached to the Dorsets. He went through heavy fighting in the Somme district in 1916 without being wounded, and was mentioned in Sir Douglas Haig's despatches for his gallantry. On 3rd October 1918, as he was advancing through the barrage to the attack, a shell dropped at his feet and killed him instantly. As one of three brothers who are all Leightonians, F. S. Brain's death is naturally very keenly felt; but his personal charm, recognised at school, at the university and in the army, was a stronger bond still; it would seem as if all men who got to know him were attracted to him.

S. F. Lennard

Full name: Samuel Fredrick Lennard
Years at L.P: 1908-1912
House: Grove
Position in military: Lieutenant, 1st and 4th Battalion
Leicestershire Regiment
Date of death: 30/03/1916 (aged 21)
Reason for death: killed in action

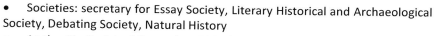

At Leighton Park

- School Sport: 1st XI cricket team, Captain of 2nd XI football

- Societies: secretary for Essay Society, Literary Historical and Archaeological Society, Debating Society, Natural History

- At the Big Social of December 1908 he did a chemistry demonstration of "the quantative synthesis of water", and played a schoolboy in a production of "Examination Day."

- Gymnastics Competition 1910: In the junior events S. F. Lennard came 1st in stall bars and boom, 2nd in horizontal bars and ropes.

- Natural History Society: "S. F. Lennard gave evidence that he had lately seen a hedgehog close beside a cow, that it may probably have been milking it."

- Cricket 1911: "S. F. Lennard promises to be a good batter and bowler. Needs more alertness in the field."

- Athletic Contest 1912: Lennard came 1st in the 100 yards.

Post Leighton Park

- "S. F. Lennard is working through the many departments of the Kettering Boot Company."

The War

-

At the outbreak of the war he joined the Leicester regiment as a private, and gained a commission in 1915. He was killed in action in March.

H. W. Ransom

Full name: Hubert William Ransom
Years at L.P: 1910-1914
House: Grove
Position in military: Second Lieutenant, Royal Flying Corps, 70th Squadron
Date of death: 27/03/1918 (aged 21)
Reason for death: killed in action

At Leighton Park
- Societies: Junior Essay Society, Camera Club
- Gymnastics Competition 1910: In the junior events Ransom came 3rd in horse.
- Athletic Sports Competition, Saturday 8th of April 1911: In the junior events Ransom came 3rd in 100 yards, 440 yards, 880 yards, and 2nd in 220 yards.
- Ransom ran in the steeplechase in 1913, he ran behind the leader for most of the race, before falling to fourth place in the final stretch.
- He was appointed prefect in September 1913.
- At the Athletic Sports Competition April 1914, Ransom came 1st in 880 yards, 2nd in steeplechase, and 3rd in mile and 440 yards.

The War
- He first saw active service as a despatch rider, delivering urgent messages between headquarters and military units, with the Armoured Cars in German South-West Africa. He then served under General Smuts in German East Africa. Returning home he obtained his commission in the Royal Flying Corps, and proceeded to the Western front, where he fell.

W. P. Southall

Full name: William Percival Southall
Years at L.P: 1912-1916
House: Grove
Position in military: Lieutenant, 64th squadron, Royal Air Force
Date of death: 28/05/1918 (aged 20)
Reason for death: shot down over enemy lines

At Leighton Park

- School Sport: 2nd XI football team, 2nd XI cricket team, Grove House football team
- Societies: Natural History Society, Debating Society, Camera Club
- Natural History Society: "A few members took some photographs, the best being a series of flower photographs by Southall."
- Southall, Ransom and Pollard were still at school at the outbreak of war.
- He won the 1914 K. H. Brooks Prize for the best set of 12 lanternslides of natural history subjects.
- At a Natural History Society meeting, Southall read a paper on "The Colour of Mammals."
- He kept a jerboa (a large eared rodent) as a pet at school.
- In 1915 Pollard and Southall joined a fruit picking camp for students of Friends' schools, in Wickhamford near Evesham, as part of the war effort. It was set up due to a shortage of professional labour in the district.
- In Camera Club, Southall was awarded 1st prize in the sports photography competition, winning a prize of 5 shillings.
- Athletic Sports Competition 1916: Southall came 1st in the high jump, with a jump of 5 foot and ½ an inch.

Post Leighton Park

- He joined the Officers' Training School Corps at Durham University.

The War

- Second Lieutenant W. P. Southall was from Edgbaston. On leaving L.P, he joined the R.A.F, and served in the 64th Squadron in France. On one occasion he came down with several bullet holes in one plane, and on another had a long fight, in which he fired some 300 rounds. A week later his aeroplane was brought down in flames over the German lines.

- He was awarded the 1914-1918 Gallantry medal.
- "Casualties among Midland Officers" Birmingham Post extract from June 1918: "Lieutenant W. Percival Southall, Royal Air Force, who was reported missing on May 28th is now reported killed in aerial combat on that date. Lieutenant Southall, who was 20 years of age, was educated at West House School, Edgbaston, and Leighton Park, Reading, and left school to join the Officers Training School Corps of Durham University. He was given his commission in July 1917, and his Wings in the following October. He went to France in March of this year. His commanding officer writes describing the circumstances under which Lieutenant Southall met his death; they were remarkable for their extraordinary gallantry: "A formation of six German machines was attempting to cross our lines to interfere with the work of our artillery machines in the neighbourhood, when Lieutenant Southall with great gallantry, attacked them single handed. The other machines went up to help but were too late to prevent him being shot down."

W. W. Pollard

Full name: Wilfred Walter Pollard
Years at L.P: 1914-1916
House: Grove
Position in military: Second Lieutenant, 206th Squadron, RAF
Date of death: 05/07/1918 (aged 19)
Reason for death: haemorrhaged from flying at great altitude

At Leighton Park

• Societies: secretary of the Literary Historical and Archaeological Society, Natural History Society, Junior Essay Society, Debating Society, played the violin in the band
• At the Mid-Term Social ,1914, Pollard played a violin solo.
• He was the scorer for the cricket team.
• In 1915 Pollard and Southall joined a fruit picking camp for students of Friends' schools as part of the war effort.
• Essay Society: Pollard read an essay on "The Black Dwarf."
• At the 1915 Grove social, in a series of scenes from school life, Pollard played one of the teachers in a scene from monthly meeting, a scene that the actual teachers thought "will leave a refreshing memory."

The War

• He joined the R.A.F, and underwent training at Hastings and Hythe. He then left for France, but was invalided home, through an attack of haemorrhage, brought on by flying at a great altitude, and died in a London hospital.

TWO UNATTRIBUTED POEMS FOUND
IN 'THE LEIGHTONIAN'

SONNET ON THE AUTUMN OF 1914

Oh turn, oh turn thy lustrous eyes away,
Spirit of Love, thy gaze cannot behold
The loathing and the malice which have sold
This piteous earth; and now each shortened day
Scatters departing fragrance round these bowers
In pleasant England, and all tranquil lie
The mist-veiled meadows, gazing at the sky-
Alas! whene'er these lovely autumn hours
Beguile my errant fancy, I but think
What peaceful pastures in a sister land
Resound with battle din, where mailed hand,
In ruthless fury plunges o'er death's brink
All noblest manhood, stains the verdant sod
With youthful blood – and in the name of God
Courage be thine and strength!
Thine aspirations
Trust! Ever welcome boyhood's princely dower!
Behold! In peaceful fellowship the nations
Bless they rich boyhood for its manhood's power.

TO LPS, JUNE 1917

The stumbling Kennet laughs its boyish way
To swell our father Thames: the Loddon flows
With smoother waters, crowned with lilies gay;
He a maturer offering bestows.

Between the streams, well builded, fair to see,
Rises a school, set where in ample ring,
Primæval trees, in nature's ecstasy,
Fulfil the annual promise of their spring.

What wealth of grass and timely fruits and flowers!
Let history tell of famed academies;
Our hearts are given to these fields of ours,
On their rich variance we feast our eyes.

Leightonians all, we play our English games
On English turf, refreshed by English rain,
Self heedless, keen for 'School'. Who blames
Our strenuous leisure? deems our efforts vain?

Each clod of earth is fraught with memories
Of earlier sportsmen's deeds with bat or ball'
Successive scholars' calmer rivalries
Some far-off boy to masters' thoughts recall.

Thus we in fellowship of sport or learning,
Herald the future, resurrect the past.
We pass, the school abides, fresh laurels earning;
The first boy victor triumphs with the last.

Yet for us present heirs of past endeavour,
A harder task stands waiting – to o'erthrow
Rank raging Ruin, that mankind for ever
Redeemed from war their common goal may know.

This be our contest! Who at ease reclines
In mankind's hour of dire extremity?
In vain too late the slothful one repines;
See man with man bound fast in enmity!

"Thy country needs thee" – 'Tis an awful cry.
Confession of a world asleep; for when
Does England not need English energy?
Was Daniel more a Daniel in the den?

Clear stands the need to view now. Nations wake
In hell, the steady goal of their ambition.
To work, young scholar, hell's dominion break,
Or all be broken in thine inanition!

CONCLUDING REFLECTIONS

Many of the Leightonians who survived the War went on to make outstanding contributions in all sectors of society, with a notably high number in the medical profession. News of their achievements was often recorded in post-war 'Leightonian' magazines. The joy of such success was tempered by the awareness of the tragic wastage of the promising young lives of their fallen Leightonian peers.

We write as a former teacher and a former pupil, and we hope that the reader will have felt able, as we have done, to empathise with these young men who lived and died a century ago. It is a form of Leightonian fellowship dislocated in time and experience, but nonetheless keenly felt.

At the outbreak of the Second World War Edgar Castle, Headmaster since 1929 wrote to Charles Evans:

I didn't think I should have to pilot Leighton Park through a war as my predecessor had to do.

On 28th July, 1946, a Service of Remembrance and Dedication to those who had died in the Second World War was held at Leighton Park. We reproduce here part of the address delivered by the Headmaster on that day. Edgar Castle's words, apposite to the First World War as much as to the Second, invite us to chastened reflection.

What did they die for – these young men whose lives were lovely and pleasant and full of promise? Did they die that you and I might have a softer life? If they died for that their death has little meaning. Did they die that the world might go on as before   – a prey to selfish men? Their death would have still less meaning if that were true. Did they die that their country might be made strong enough to dominate the weak? Knowing them we know also that they did not die for that.

We who know them so well know that they died for great ideals without which life as should be lived becomes impossible.

In dying they pass on to us the inextinguishable torch of those who died for great ideals.

ACKNOWLEDGEMENTS

The authors wish to thank a number of people who have given their encouragement and assistance in various ways.

Penny Wallington, Director of Old Leightonian Relations, has given extensive support at each stage of this production and we wish to record our special thanks to her for her invaluable help.

Ken Sullivan's role as publisher and guide has been indispensable.

Conservatree Print & Design and Richard Wallington for special assistance with the design and production of the book.

We also thank, for a variety of reasons:

Isabel Allinson, Graham Carter, Nathan Dracott, Tom Gillmor , Cathy Harman, Henry Ireland, Albert Saelens, Jane Smith, David Wallace, Nigel Williams.

The very helpful staff at Mary Evans Picture Library, University of Birmingham Cadbury Research Library, The Liddle Collection at the Brotherton Library, University of Leeds, The Library at Friends House, London.

Picture Credits:

© Mary Evans Picture Library (www.maryevans.com)

© Illustrated London News Ltd / Mary Evans

© Robert Hunt Library / Mary Evans

© Pump Park Photography / Mary Evans

© National Army Museum / Mary Evans

IN REMEMBRANCE

After the War, the Old Leightonians established a scholarship fund to help the children of those of their friends who had died to be educated at Leighton Park. They raised the money to pay for the Memorial Garden and the sundial outside Peckover. The Memorial Tablet, to be found inside Peckover, is also a gift from the Old Leightonians.

THEY DIED FOR GREAT IDEALS